MW01254242

Yellow Umbrella Books are published by Capstone Press
151 Good Counsel Drive, P.O. Box 669, Mankato, Minnesota 56002
http://www.capstone-press.com

Library of Congress Cataloging-in-Publication Data
Bauer, David.
  Let's Sort / by David Bauer.
    p. cm.—(Math)
  Includes Index.
Summary: Introduces things that can be sorted by color, shape, or size.
  ISBN 0-7368-2014-0 (hardcover : alk. paper)
  1. English language—Set theory—Juvenile literature.   I. Title. II. Series.
QA248 .B384 2003
428.2—dc21

                                                          2003000931

Editorial Credits
Mary Lindeen, Editorial Director; Jennifer Van Voorst, Editor; Wanda Winch, Photo Researcher

Photo Credits
Cover: Comstock; Title Page: Jim Foell/Capstone Press; Page 2: Phil Bulgasch/Capstone Press;
Page 3: Jim Foell/Capstone Press; Page 4 - Page 15: Phil Bulgasch/Capstone Press; Page 16: Jim
Foell/Capstone Press

1 2 3 4 5 6 08 07 06 05 04 03

Let's Sort

by David Bauer

Consultants: David Olson, Director of Undergraduate Studies, and Tamara Olson, Associate Professor, Department of Mathematical Sciences, Michigan Technological University

Yellow Umbrella Books

an imprint of Capstone Press
Mankato, Minnesota

You can sort things in many ways.

You can sort by color, shape, or size.

Let's sort by color.

Some towels are dark colored. Some towels are light colored.

Let's sort by color again.

Some apples are green.
Some apples are red.

Let's sort by shape.

Some crackers are round.
Some crackers are square.

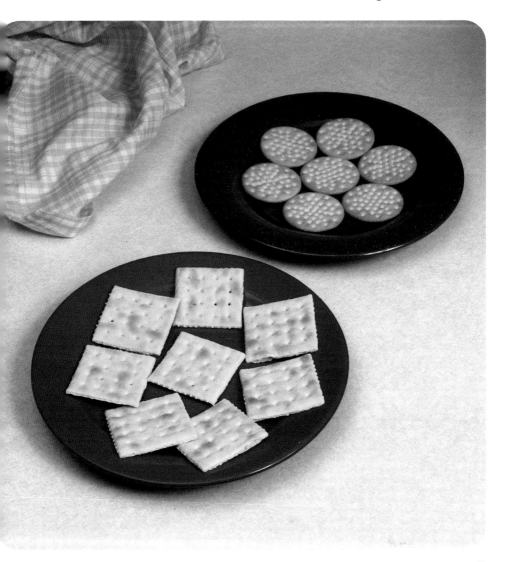

Let's sort by shape again.

Some blocks are squares.
Some blocks are triangles.

Let's sort by size.

Some teddy bears are big.
Some teddy bears are small.

Let's sort by size again.

Some balls are big.
Some balls are small.

How would you sort these crayons?

Words to Know/Index

Word Count: 100
Early-Intervention Level: 6